W9-CTI-491

WOMEN'S SUFFRAGE

BY DUCHESS HARRIS, JD, PHD

Core Library

Cover image: Suffragists hand out flyers promoting women's suffrage.

An Imprint of Abdo Publishing
abdopublishing.com

abdopublishing.com

Published by Abdo Publishing, a division of ABDO, PO Box 398166, Minneapolis, Minnesota 55439. Copyright © 2018 by Abdo Consulting Group, Inc. International copyrights reserved in all countries. No part of this book may be reproduced in any form without written permission from the publisher. Core Library™ is a trademark and logo of Abdo Publishing.

Printed in the United States of America, North Mankato, Minnesota
092017
012018

Cover Photo: Bain News Service/Library of Congress
Interior Photos: Bain News Service/Library of Congress, 1; Schomburg Center for Research in Black Culture/Photographs and Prints Division/The New York Public Library, 4–5; Bettmann/Getty Images, 7; Victorian Traditions/Shutterstock Images, 10–11; S. B. Morton/Frank Leslie's illustrated newspaper/Library of Congress, 14; Interim Archives/Archive Photos/Getty Images, 16–17; B. West Clinedinst/Frank Leslie's Illustrated Newspaper/Library of Congress, 21; H. B. Lindsley/Library of Congress, 22–23; Everett Historical/Shutterstock Images, 28–29; Paul Thompson/Topical Press Agency/Hulton Archive/Getty Images, 31; Red Line Editorial, 34, 41; National Photo Company Collection/Library of Congress, 36–37

Editor: Marie Pearson
Imprint Designer: Maggie Villaume
Series Design Direction: Claire Mathiowetz
Contributor: Valerie Bodden

Publisher's Cataloging-in-Publication Data

Names: Harris, Duchess, author.
Title: Women's suffrage / by Duchess Harris.
Description: Minneapolis, Minnesota : Abdo Publishing, 2018. | Series: Protest movements | Includes online resources and index.
Identifiers: LCCN 2017947130 | ISBN 9781532113994 (lib.bdg.) | ISBN 9781532152870 (ebook)
Subjects: LCSH: Suffragists--Juvenile literature. | Women--Suffrage--United States--History--Juvenile literature. | Voting--United States--Juvenile literature.
Classification: DDC 324.6230973--dc23
LC record available at https://lccn.loc.gov/2017947130

CONTENTS

SENECA FALLS

T he roads leading to Seneca Falls, New York, were crowded. It was the morning of July 19, 1848. People on foot and in horse-drawn wagons traveled toward the small town's Wesleyan Chapel. They had seen a notice in the *Seneca County Courier* five days earlier. It announced a two-day convention about women's rights.

Elizabeth Cady Stanton and Lucretia Mott organized the convention. They had feared no one would show up. But more than 300 people crowded the chapel's benches. The first day of the meeting was only for women. Approximately 40 men also showed up. The organizers allowed them to stay. The morning's

One of the women's suffrage movement's founders was Lucretia Mott.

NEW LIFE FOR WESLEYAN CHAPEL

The Wesleyan Chapel in Seneca Falls was sold in 1871. Over the years, the building served as a garage and Laundromat. In 1985, the National Park Service purchased the site. Very little of the original structure remained. The park service rebuilt the chapel in 2011. It opened the Women's Rights National Historical Park on the site.

program included speeches by Stanton and Mott. Stanton told her listeners it was wrong that women did not have suffrage, or the right to vote.

A DECLARATION

Stanton presented a document she and the other leaders had written. They called it the Declaration of Rights and Sentiments.

The document said that all men and women were created equal. It listed 18 injustices women suffered. Among them was that women did not have the right to attend college. Women were paid less and kept out

An artist depicted Stanton speaking at the convention.

YOUNG SIGNER

Nineteen-year-old Charlotte Woodward saw the announcement for the Seneca Falls Convention in the newspaper. She made plans with friends to attend. Woodward feared she and her friends would be the only women there. They were relieved to meet plenty of other women there. Woodward sat in the back row listening to the speeches and debate. Then she signed the Declaration of Rights and Sentiments. She was the only signer still alive in 1920. That's the year the 19th Amendment gave women the right to vote.

of many jobs. They were denied the right to vote.

The Declaration also included 11 resolutions that offered solutions. The next day, those at the convention voted on the resolutions. The most controversial was demanding the right to vote. Many, including Mott, felt it was too soon to ask for suffrage. But Stanton and others believed women could only be equal if they could vote for their own leaders. In the end, convention attendees voted to accept all 11 resolutions. A total of 68 women and 32 men signed the Declaration.

BIRTH OF A MOVEMENT

The Seneca Falls Convention was the first major meeting held to discuss women's rights. But it wasn't the last. After Seneca Falls, women across the country became involved. They worked to win the right for women to vote. It would take them 72 years. In the process, they would change the shape of American politics.

EXPLORE ONLINE

Chapter One covers the Seneca Falls Convention. The website below provides a firsthand account of the meeting. How is the information from the website the same as the information in Chapter One? What new information did you learn from the website?

SENECA FALLS CONVENTION

abdocorelibrary.com/womens-suffrage

BEFORE WOMEN'S RIGHTS

I n 1787, 55 male delegates from the newly independent United States met in Philadelphia, Pennsylvania. They wrote a constitution for the country. They gave little thought to women's rights as they wrote it. They saw women as dependent on men. As a result, women had few rights. They could not vote or hold public office. They could not sign contracts or serve on juries. When a woman married, her money and property became her husband's. Black women had fewer rights than

The US founders only had white men in mind when forming the country.

FUTURE FIRST LADY

Abigail Adams was the wife of future president John Adams. She wrote him a letter about women's rights in 1776. In it, she told him not to give husbands too much power. She warned that if women were ignored, they would start a rebellion. She said women without a voice in the government would not have to follow its laws. Adams's ideas were ahead of her time. They were later adopted by the women's rights movement.

white women. Many were enslaved.

A woman's place was seen as being at home. She cleaned, cooked, and raised her children. Few girls received an education. Girls from wealthier families were sometimes educated. But their lessons focused on painting, singing, and learning French. Most women accepted their place in society. But a few pushed back. In 1792, British author Mary Wollstonecraft argued in favor of equal rights for women, including in education.

SLOW CHANGES

In the early 1800s, education became available to more women. In 1833, Oberlin College in Ohio became the first college to allow women. The first women's college, Mount Holyoke, opened in 1837. The school trained many women to become teachers. But educated women could not hold many other jobs. They could not enter the fields of law or medicine.

For poorer women, education still was not an option. Many went to work in the nation's factories. They faced long hours, low pay, and poor safety standards. They received less pay than men for the same work.

SAME WORK, LOWER PAY

In the 1830s, many women became teachers. But female teachers were paid much less than male teachers. Susan B. Anthony made $2.50 a week as a teacher. Male teachers in her school earned $10 a week. In 1851, male teachers in Connecticut earned $20 a month. Female teachers made only $8.69.

Some women in the temperance movement sang hymns outside of bars.

REFORM WORK

Factories began to grow in the 1800s. Many items could now be bought, not made. Stores sold cloth, soap, bread, and other items. Upper-class women no longer had to make these things at home. This gave them free time. Many used that time to join reform movements. Thousands of women became involved in the temperance movement. They tried to get the government to outlaw alcohol. Some groups refused to let women join. So women formed their own societies.

Many women also joined the abolition, or antislavery, movement. They held meetings, conducted petition drives, and gave speeches. Female speakers often faced ridicule. In some cases, they were met with violence. This treatment made many women aware of their low position in society.

In 1840, American abolitionists traveled to the World Anti-Slavery Convention in London, England. Among them were a few women, including Stanton and Mott. But many male delegates did not want women to participate in the meeting. The women could listen. But they could not speak at the convention. That night, Stanton and Mott vowed to hold a women's rights convention.

FURTHER EVIDENCE

Chapter Two talks about women's roles in early American history. Identify one of the chapter's main points. What key evidence supports this point? Read the article at the website below. Does the information on the website support the main point of the chapter? Does it present new evidence?

WOMEN'S HISTORY IN AMERICA

abdocorelibrary.com/womens-suffrage

LAUNCHING A MOVEMENT

Mott's and Stanton's plans for a women's rights conference led to the Seneca Falls Convention of 1848. The leaders expected a positive response from the public. But they were mocked in many newspapers. Church leaders criticized them as well.

Yet the women's rights movement gained momentum. In 1850, the first National Women's Rights Convention was held in Worcester, Massachusetts. As many as 1,000 people attended. National conventions were held almost every year for the next ten years. Topics included women's education and

Mott faced insults and physical harm while she worked for women's suffrage and to end slavery.

employment. Activists also debated marriage laws and voting rights.

By the second national convention, several women had risen within the movement. Among them were Stanton, Mott, Susan B. Anthony, and Lucy Stone. Many men also joined the movement. These included William Lloyd Garrison and Frederick Douglass.

REFORM METHODS

The movement's leaders decided not to form a national women's rights organization. They feared doing so would cause conflict among reformers with different priorities. They also worried it would restrict individuals' creativity in making and carrying out new reform efforts. Instead, they promoted state and local women's rights groups. These groups held local conventions. They studied issues related to women's rights and shared their findings.

Many of the most prominent reformers gave lectures. At a time before television and radio, lectures were a popular form of entertainment. Stone's lecture tours made her one of the most famous women of her era. Many women also wrote newspaper articles and essays. Some started their own newspapers.

Many who supported women's rights continued to face resistance. Some people attended conventions just to disrupt speeches. Some threw stones, eggs, and rotten fruit at the speakers.

PETITION DRIVES

Conventions and lectures helped raise awareness of

FASHION FORWARD

In the mid-1800s, an upper-class woman's outfit could weigh as much as 12 pounds (5.4 kg). It consisted of layers of long skirts puffed out by hoops. Waist up, women wore tight undergarments called corsets. The heavy, uncomfortable clothing made movement difficult. After the Seneca Falls Convention, some reformers wore pantaloons, or bloomers, under shorter skirts. This gave them freedom to move comfortably. But it caused a public outcry. People began to pay more attention to the women's clothing than their message. Most went back to wearing traditional clothing.

the women's rights movement. But they couldn't bring about change on their own. So women held petition drives. They collected the signatures of those in favor of suffrage. Then they presented their petitions to government officials.

Petition drives were often long and tiring. Volunteers went from house to house, asking residents to sign. Many people slammed doors in their faces. Those who listened were often unwilling to sign. Some said women had enough rights. Even with many signatures, there was no guarantee a petition

Women collect signatures during a petition drive. They worked long hours to gather signatures.

would bring about change. Government officials still often voted against reform.

EARLY SUCCESSES

But the women's rights movement had some early successes. By 1860, 16 states had given married women more property rights. More women's colleges opened. Women began to enter fields such as medicine. In a few places, women even won some local voting rights. In Kentucky, widowed mothers could vote in school board elections.

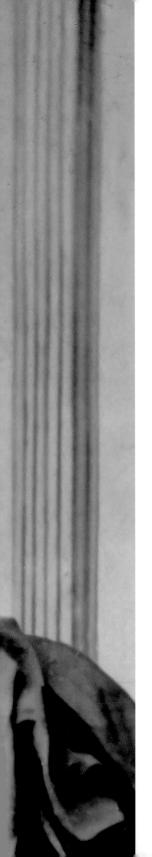

DIVISIONS

The American Civil War (1861–1865) broke out in April 1861. The northern states, or the Union, fought the southern states, or the Confederacy. The central issue was the practice of slavery. The southern states wanted to preserve slavery. They broke away from the United States to do so. The northern states fought to reunite the nation.

During the war, the women's rights movement came to a halt. Women around the country helped the war effort. More than 3,000 women served as nurses in the war. Others rolled bandages and collected food for

Harriet Tubman was an abolitionist. She served as a spy and as a cook and nurse for the Union Army during the Civil War.

troops. Some even served as spies. They hid letters in their corsets.

Women also took on new tasks at home. Many ran their husbands' farms. Others filled in for men in factories. They helped make uniforms, boots, and weapons.

SPLIT

The Civil War came to an end in 1865. Slavery was abolished, or ended. Many women thought winning the vote would be easy now. Their work in the war effort had been valuable.

But activists found themselves divided over the 15th Amendment to the US Constitution. This amendment would give African-American men the right to vote. Stanton and Anthony opposed it because it didn't include women. In 1869, they formed the National Woman Suffrage Association (NWSA). Others, including Stone, supported the amendment. They created the American Woman Suffrage Association

(AWSA). The two organizations used different methods to achieve their goals. The AWSA focused on individual states. The NWSA sought a national women's suffrage amendment.

By the 1870s, some women were ready to take more drastic measures. Some refused to pay their taxes. Others tried to register to vote but were turned away. In 1872, Anthony and 14 other women voted in Rochester, New York. Anthony was arrested. She was found guilty of voting without the right to do so. She was fined $100, which she refused to pay.

WESTERN WOMEN

Western states were the first to grant women suffrage for several reasons. Women in the West were more likely to be seen as men's equals. They faced the same hard frontier life as men. They often helped with traditional men's duties. Men also greatly outnumbered women in the West. Women's votes were unlikely to impact the outcome of an election.

SMALL ADVANCES

By 1870, the territories of Wyoming and Utah had granted women's suffrage. In 1893, Colorado became the first state to give women voting rights. Idaho followed three years later. Wyoming and Utah became states in the 1890s. This brought the total number of suffrage states to four.

In 1886, the US Senate voted on a suffrage amendment for the first time. It was defeated. The amendment was brought to Congress almost every year until 1896. It was defeated each time.

STRAIGHT TO THE
SOURCE

In 1872, Susan B. Anthony was arrested for voting. She traveled the country delivering a stirring speech that defended her right to vote:

> It was we, the people, not we, the white male citizens, nor yet we, the male citizens, but we, the whole people, who formed this Union. . . . But, it is urged, the use of the masculine pronouns he, his, and him . . . is proof that only men were meant to be included. . . . If you insist on this version of the letter of the law, we shall insist that you be consistent, . . . which would compel you to exempt women from taxation for the support of the government, and from penalties for the violation of laws. . . . There is no she, or her, or hers, in the tax laws. . . .

> Source: Susan B. Anthony. "Is It a Crime for a Citizen of the United States to Vote?" in Kathryn Cullen-Du Pont, ed. *American Women Activists' Writings: An Anthology, 1637–2002*. New York: Cooper Square Press, 2002. Print. 168–169.

Back It Up
The author of this passage uses evidence to support a point. Write a paragraph describing the point the author is making. Then write down two or three pieces of evidence the author uses to make the point.

STRAIGHT TO THE
SOURCE

After the vote was won, people did not see signs of immediate change. Carrie Chapman Catt described suffrage as part of the larger women's rights movement:

> *Every woman discharged from the suffrage campaign merely stepped back into the ranks of the broader woman movement from which she and her predecessors emerged some seventy-five years ago with the definite object of eliminating one discrimination against women. . . . What is the woman movement and what is its aim? It is a demand for equality of opportunity between the sexes. It means that when and if a woman is as well qualified as a man to fill a position, she shall have an equal and unprejudiced chance to secure it.*

Source: Carrie Chapman Catt. "Woman Suffrage Only an Episode in Age-Old Movement," in DeLuzio, Crista, ed. *Women's Rights: People and Perspectives.* Santa Barbara, CA: ABC-CLIO, 2010. Print. 237–238.

Consider Your Audience

Adapt this passage for a different audience, such as your principal or friends. Write a blog post conveying this same information for the new audience. How does your post differ from the original text and why?

BEYOND THE VOTE

With suffrage passed, women continued to work for other rights. In 1923, Paul began pushing Congress to pass an Equal Rights Amendment (ERA). The ERA stated that a person's rights could not be denied because of gender. Congress discussed the amendment several times over the years. But it did not gain enough support.

RENEWED ACTIVISM

By the 1960s, more women had entered the workforce. But they were paid approximately 60 percent of what men made. In 1963, Betty

Paul, *left*, later became an advisor to the US Women's Bureau, which promotes women's rights.

Friedan published *The Feminine Mystique*. The book urged women to pursue meaningful careers. A new women's rights movement emerged. It focused on inequalities in pay and employment. The movement gained some early successes. In 1963, Congress passed the Equal Pay Act. This law prevented gender discrimination in pay.

Another important social movement was happening in this era: the civil rights movement. African Americans worked to gain rights and protections under the law. One of these was the right to vote. African-American men and women frequently had their voting rights denied or restricted. The work of the two movements sometimes overlapped. The Civil Rights Act of 1964 prohibited job discrimination based on race or gender.

WOMEN'S LIBERATION

Some women formed the women's liberation movement in the late 1960s. They held marches, demonstrations, and pickets. They focused on changing people's views

IMPORTANT
DATES

1848
The Seneca Falls Convention, which opens on July 19, begins the women's suffrage movement.

1850
The first National Women's Rights Convention is held in Worcester, Massachusetts.

1869
The National Woman Suffrage Association (NWSA) and American Woman Suffrage Association (AWSA) are formed.

1886
Congress votes on a suffrage amendment for the first time.

1890
The NWSA and AWSA merge to form the National American Woman Suffrage Association.

1919
The 19th Amendment passes Congress on June 4 and is ratified 14 months later.

2016
Hillary Clinton becomes the first woman to win a major party's presidential nomination.

STOP AND
THINK

Tell the Tale

Chapter One of this book discusses the Seneca Falls Convention. Imagine you are planning your own convention. Write 200 words about what your convention will discuss. How will you let people know about it?

Surprise Me

Chapter Two discusses women's lives in early America. After reading this book, what two or three facts about women's lives did you find most surprising? Write a few sentences about each fact. Why did you find each fact surprising?

Dig Deeper

After reading this book, what questions do you still have about women's suffrage? With an adult's help, find a few reliable sources that can help you answer your questions. Write a paragraph about what you learned.

GLOSSARY

amendment
an addition or change to the US Constitution

constitution
a document stating the system of laws of a nation or state and the rights guaranteed to its people

delegate
a person given the job of speaking for or representing others, often at a convention

inauguration
a ceremony through which an official is placed into office

petition
a formal written request signed by a large number of people

picket
to stand outside a building, often holding signs, as a form of protest

ratify
to formally approve

reform
to change the way things are done to address an injustice

resolution
a declaration from a governing body of its intent

territory
a region of the United States that is not a state but is overseen by a governor

ONLINE
RESOURCES

To learn more about women's suffrage, visit our free resource websites below.

Visit **abdocorelibrary.com** for free Common Core resources for teachers and students, including vetted activities, multimedia, and booklinks, for deeper subject comprehension.

Visit **abdobooklinks.com** for free additional online weblinks for further learning. These links are routinely monitored and updated to provide the most current information available.

LEARN
MORE

Conley, Kate. *Voting and Elections*. Minneapolis, MN: Abdo Publishing, 2017.

Peppas, Lynn. *Women's Suffrage*. New York: Crabtree Publishing Company, 2016.

ABOUT THE
AUTHOR

Duchess Harris, JD, PhD

Professor Harris is the chair of the American Studies Department at Macalester College. The author and coauthor of four books (*Hidden Human Computers: The Black Women of NASA* and *Black Lives Matter* with Sue Bradford Edwards, *Racially Writing the Republic: Racists, Race Rebels, and Transformations of American Identity* with Bruce Baum, and *Black Feminist Politics from Kennedy to Clinton/Obama*), she has been an associate editor for *Litigation News*, the American Bar Association Section's quarterly flagship publication, and was the first editor-in-chief of *Law Raza Journal*, an interactive online race and the law journal for William Mitchell College of Law.

She has earned a PhD in American Studies from the University of Minnesota and a Juris Doctorate from William Mitchell College of Law.

INDEX